# Better Homes and Gardens.

# Chicken

## Easy Everyday Recipe Library

BETTER HOMES AND GARDENS® BOOKS

Des Moines, Iowa

EASY EVERYDAY RECIPE LIBRARY
Better Homes and Gardens® Books, An imprint of Meredith® Books
Published for Creative World Enterprises LP, West Chester, Pennsylvania
www.creativeworldcooking.com

*Chicken*
Project Editors: Spectrum Communication Services, Inc.
Project Designers: Seif Visual Communications
Copy Chief: Catherine Hamrick
Copy and Production Editor: Terri Fredrickson
Contributing Proofreaders: Kathy Eastman, Susan J. Kling
Electronic Production Coordinator: Paula Forest
Editorial and Design Assistants: Judy Bailey, Mary Lee Gavin, Karen Schirm
Test Kitchen Director: Lynn Blanchard
Production Director: Douglas M. Johnston
Production Managers: Pam Kvitne, Marjorie J. Schenkelberg

Meredith® Books
Editor in Chief: James D. Blume
Design Director: Matt Strelecki
Managing Editor: Gregory H. Kayko

Director, Sales & Marketing, Retail: Michael A. Peterson
Director, Sales & Marketing, Special Markets: Rita McMullen
Director, Sales & Marketing, Home & Garden Center Channel: Ray Wolf
Director, Operations: George A. Susral

Vice President, General Manager: Jamie L. Martin

*Better Homes and Gardens® Magazine*
Editor in Chief: Jean LemMon
Executive Food Editor: Nancy Byal

Meredith Publishing Group
President, Publishing Group: Christopher M. Little
Vice President, Consumer Marketing & Development: Hal Oringer

Meredith Corporation
Chairman and Chief Executive Officer: William T. Kerr

Chairman of the Executive Committee: E. T. Meredith III

Creative World Enterprises LP
Publisher: Richard J. Petrone
Design Consultants to Creative World Enterprises: Coastline Studios, Orlando, Florida

All of us at Better Homes and Gardens® Books are dedicated to providing you with the information and ideas you need to create delicious foods. We welcome your comments and suggestions. Write to us at: Better Homes and Gardens Books, Cookbook Editorial Department, 1716 Locust St., Des Moines, Iowa 50309-3023.

Our seal assures you that every recipe in *Chicken* has been tested in the Better Homes and Gardens® Test Kitchen. This means that each recipe is practical and reliable, and meets our high standards of taste appeal. We guarantee your satisfaction with this book for as long as you own it.

*Cover photo: Chicken & Prosciutto Roll-Ups*
*(see recipe, page 40)*

What characteristics would you wish for in a "perfect" food? Perhaps tasty, appealing, nutritious, economical, and versatile? Then chicken just may be a wish come true. It boasts each of these virtues!

Chicken's well-rounded flavor appeals to a wide range of tastes. And it's a wholesome source of low-fat protein, as well as a good food bargain. And as for ways to cook it… well, imagination is the only limit. From the tasteful simplicity of a roasted bird to the sheer elegance of a stuffed boneless breast, chicken offers something for everyone.

## CONTENTS

# Keys-Style Citrus Chicken

*The tropical-island-inspired cooking of the Florida Keys draws on the best of both worlds. Here, it combines fresh Florida citrus with the Caribbean penchant for fiery peppers. Soak up the delicious juice with hot cooked rice.*

4 medium skinless, boneless chicken breast halves (about 1 pound total)
2 or 3 cloves garlic, peeled and thinly sliced
1 tablespoon butter or margarine
1 teaspoon finely shredded lime peel
2 tablespoons lime juice
¼ teaspoon ground ginger
⅛ teaspoon crushed red pepper
1 orange
Hot cooked rice (optional)
Lime wedges (optional)

Rinse chicken; pat dry with paper towels. In a large skillet cook chicken and garlic in butter or margarine over medium heat for 8 to 10 minutes or till chicken is tender and no longer pink, turning chicken once and stirring garlic occasionally.

Meanwhile, in a small bowl combine lime peel, lime juice, ginger, and red pepper; set aside. Peel orange. Reserving juice, cut orange in half lengthwise, then cut crosswise into slices. Add any reserved orange juice and the lime juice mixture to skillet.

Place orange slices on top of chicken. Cover and cook for 1 to 2 minutes or till heated through.

To serve, spoon any reserved drippings over chicken. If desired, serve with cooked rice and garnish with lime wedges. Makes 4 servings.

*Nutrition information per serving: 167 calories, 22 g protein, 5 g carbohydrate, 6 g fat (3 g saturated), 67 mg cholesterol, 84 mg sodium.*

## Learning About Limes

If a recipe calls for lime peel or lime juice, keep in mind that one lime will give you about 1½ teaspoons of grated peel and 2 tablespoons of juice. When you're looking for limes in the supermarket, select fruit that is brightly colored, heavy for its size, and free of blemishes.

# Quick Chicken Molé

*Continue the Mexican theme by serving warm flour tortillas, tomato salsa seasoned with chopped cilantro, and sliced oranges layered with coconut for dessert.*

6  medium chicken breast halves
    (about 3 pounds total)
2  tablespoons olive oil or cooking oil
1  small onion, chopped
1  clove garlic, minced
1½  teaspoons chili powder
1  teaspoon sesame seed
¼  teaspoon salt
¼  teaspoon ground cumin
¼  teaspoon ground cinnamon
1  small tomato, chopped
1  tomatillo, peeled and cut into
    wedges, or 1 small tomato,
    chopped
½  cup chicken broth
½  cup tomato sauce
2  tablespoons raisins
2  teaspoons unsweetened cocoa
    powder
    Several dashes bottled hot pepper
    sauce
    Hot cooked rice
    Toasted pumpkin seed or slivered
    almonds (optional)

Skin chicken. Rinse chicken; pat dry with paper towels. In a large skillet cook chicken in hot oil over medium heat about 10 minutes or till chicken is lightly browned, turning to brown evenly. Add onion, garlic, chili powder, sesame seed, salt, cumin, and cinnamon. Cook and stir for 30 seconds.

Stir in tomato, tomatillo, chicken broth, tomato sauce, raisins, cocoa powder, and hot pepper sauce. Bring to boiling; reduce heat. Simmer, uncovered, about 15 minutes or till chicken is tender and no longer pink. Using a slotted spoon, remove chicken. Simmer sauce for 4 to 5 minutes or to desired consistency.

To serve, spoon sauce over chicken and rice. If desired, sprinkle with pumpkin seed or almonds. Makes 6 servings.

*Nutrition information per serving: 367 calories, 33 g protein, 37 g carbohydrate, 9 g fat (2 g saturated), 76 mg cholesterol, 543 mg sodium.*

## Garlic Know-How

Working with garlic is easy if you keep a few hints in mind. Loosen the garlic skin quickly by crushing each clove with the flat side of a chef's knife. The skin will slip off. To mince the peeled garlic, place it in a garlic press or use a sharp knife to cut it into tiny pieces. If you prefer, use bottled minced garlic (usually found in your supermarket's produce section) instead of the cloves.

# Curried Chicken Thighs

*You can also use skinless, boneless chicken thighs in this recipe. Just reduce the cooking time to 10 minutes after adding the chicken broth.*

8  chicken thighs (about 2½ pounds total)
2  tablespoons cooking oil
1  cup sliced fresh mushrooms
1  medium onion, chopped (½ cup)
1  clove garlic, minced
3  to 4 teaspoons curry powder
¼  teaspoon salt
¼  teaspoon ground cinnamon
¾  cup chicken broth
1  medium apple, cored and chopped
1  cup half-and-half, light cream, or milk
2  tablespoons all-purpose flour
3  cups hot cooked rice
   Assorted condiments: raisins, chopped hard-cooked egg, peanuts, chopped tomato, chopped green sweet pepper, toasted coconut, chutney, cut-up fruits (optional)

Skin chicken. Rinse chicken; pat dry with paper towels. In a 10-inch skillet cook chicken in hot oil over medium heat about 10 minutes or till lightly browned, turning to brown evenly. Remove chicken. If necessary, add 1 tablespoon additional cooking oil to skillet.

Add mushrooms, onion, and garlic to skillet; cook till vegetables are tender. Add curry powder, salt, and cinnamon; cook and stir for 1 minute. Add chicken broth and apple. Return chicken to skillet. Bring to boiling; reduce heat. Cover and simmer about 15 minutes or till chicken is tender and no longer pink.

Transfer chicken to platter; keep warm. Stir the half-and-half, light cream, or milk into the flour. Stir into pan juices. Cook and stir till thickened and bubbly. Cook and stir for 1 minute more. Spoon some sauce over chicken. Pass remaining sauce. Serve with rice and, if desired, pass condiments. Makes 4 servings.

*Nutrition information per serving: 695 calories, 54 g protein, 45 g carbohydrate, 32 g fat (10 g saturated), 158 mg cholesterol, 829 mg sodium.*

# Citrus Chicken

*Grab your skillet and this recipe when you need a quick meal for guests. To complete the meal, toss mixed greens with a light vinaigrette and end with a citrus-flavored sorbet.*

4   medium skinless, boneless chicken breast halves (about 1 pound total)

2   teaspoons finely shredded orange peel

1   cup orange juice

¼   cup balsamic vinegar or white wine vinegar

1   tablespoon cornstarch

2   teaspoons honey

1   teaspoon instant chicken bouillon granules

    Dash white pepper

2   cups sliced fresh shiitake or button mushrooms

2   tablespoons margarine or butter

8   ounces packaged dried tomato and/or plain linguine, cooked

    Chives (optional)

    Orange slices, halved (optional)

Rinse chicken; pat dry with paper towels. Place each half between 2 pieces of plastic wrap. Working from center to edges, pound lightly with the flat side of a meat mallet to ⅛-inch thickness. Remove plastic wrap.

In small bowl stir together the orange peel, orange juice, vinegar, cornstarch, honey, bouillon granules, and pepper. Set aside.

In a large skillet cook the mushrooms in margarine or butter over medium heat till tender; remove. In the same skillet cook the chicken about 4 minutes or till tender and no longer pink, turning once. Remove; keep warm. Return mushrooms to skillet. Stir orange juice mixture; add to mushrooms. Cook and stir till thickened and bubbly. Cook and stir for 2 minutes more. Serve chicken and sauce over linguine. If desired, garnish with chives and orange slices. Makes 4 servings.

*Nutrition information per serving: 434 calories, 25 g protein, 62 g carbohydrate, 9 g fat (2 g saturated), 45 mg cholesterol, 329 mg sodium.*

# Chicken with Peas and Potatoes

*Save clean-up time with this chicken meal-in-a-skillet featuring vegetables in a rosemary-scented sauce.*

1  2½- to 3-pound cut up broiler-fryer chicken or 3 pounds chicken thighs
2  tablespoons margarine or butter
1  pound small new potatoes, quartered
¾  cup chicken broth
1  teaspoon dried rosemary, crushed
¼  teaspoon pepper
1  10-ounce package frozen peas
4  green onions, thinly sliced
¼  cup snipped parsley
1  8-ounce carton dairy sour cream
2  tablespoons all-purpose flour
   Tomato slices (optional)
   Fresh rosemary sprigs (optional)

If desired, skin chicken. Rinse chicken; pat dry with paper towels. In a 12-inch skillet cook the chicken in margarine over medium heat about 15 minutes or till browned, turning to brown evenly. Add potatoes, broth, dried rosemary, and pepper. Bring to boiling; reduce heat. Cover and simmer for 30 minutes.

Add peas, green onions, and ¼ cup parsley to skillet. Cover and simmer about 10 minutes more or till the chicken and potatoes are tender and chicken is no longer pink. Using a slotted spoon, transfer chicken and vegetables to platter; keep warm.

Stir together the sour cream and flour; stir into broth mixture. Cook and stir till thickened and bubbly. Cook and stir for 1 minute more. Spoon over chicken and vegetables. If desired, garnish with tomatoes and fresh rosemary. Makes 6 servings.

*Nutrition information per serving: 491 calories, 34 g protein, 28 g carbohydrate, 27 g fat (10 g saturated), 106 mg cholesterol, 286 mg sodium.*

# Chicken and Vegetable Skillet

*Try this combination another time with angel hair pasta and a sprinkle of freshly grated Parmesan cheese.*

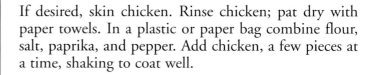

| | |
|---|---|
| 1 | 2½- to 3-pound cut up broiler-fryer chicken |
| ¼ | cup all-purpose flour |
| ½ | teaspoon salt |
| ½ | teaspoon paprika |
| ¼ | teaspoon pepper |
| 2 | tablespoons cooking oil |
| ½ | cup chopped onion |
| 2 | cloves garlic, minced |
| 1 | tablespoon grated gingerroot |
| ¾ | cup chicken broth |
| 1 | pound fresh asparagus, cut into 1-inch pieces |
| 3 | yellow summer squash and/or zucchini, cut into 1-inch chunks |
| 8 | ounces fresh mushrooms, thickly sliced (3 cups) |
| 2 | red or green sweet peppers, cut into 1-inch strips |
| ¼ | cup dry sherry |
| 2 | tablespoons soy sauce |
| 2 | teaspoons cornstarch |
| | Hot cooked orzo, rice, or noodles |

If desired, skin chicken. Rinse chicken; pat dry with paper towels. In a plastic or paper bag combine flour, salt, paprika, and pepper. Add chicken, a few pieces at a time, shaking to coat well.

In a 12-inch skillet cook the chicken in hot oil over medium heat about 10 minutes or till lightly browned, turning to brown evenly. Remove chicken. If necessary, add 1 tablespoon additional oil to skillet.

Add the onion, garlic, and gingerroot to skillet. Cook for 4 to 5 minutes or till onion is tender. Carefully stir in chicken broth. Return chicken to skillet.

Bring to boiling; reduce heat. Cover and simmer about 15 minutes or till chicken is tender and no longer pink. Spoon off excess fat.

Add asparagus, squash, mushrooms, and sweet peppers. In a measuring cup combine the dry sherry, soy sauce, and cornstarch; stir into chicken mixture.

Return to boiling; reduce heat. Cover and simmer for 5 to 10 minutes more or till vegetables are crisp-tender. Serve with orzo, rice, or noodles. Makes 4 to 6 servings.

*Nutrition information per serving: 621 calories, 51 g protein, 33 g carbohydrate, 31 g fat (7 g saturated), 134 mg cholesterol, 1,069 mg sodium.*

# Chicken Paprika

*For more flavor, we suggest the Hungarian paprika—it comes in both hot and sweet versions.*

8  ounces fresh mushrooms, sliced
   (3 cups)
1  medium onion, chopped (½ cup)
2  cloves garlic, minced
¼  cup margarine or butter
2  to 3 teaspoons Hungarian paprika
   or paprika
¼  teaspoon pepper
2  cups cubed cooked chicken
   (10 ounces)
1  14½-ounce can chicken broth
2  tablespoons tomato paste
1  8-ounce carton dairy sour cream or
   light dairy sour cream
3  tablespoons all-purpose flour
   Hot cooked wide noodles
   Parsley sprig (optional)

In a 10-inch skillet cook the mushrooms, onion, and garlic in margarine or butter over medium heat about 5 minutes or till vegetables are tender. Stir in paprika and pepper. Cook and stir for 1 minute more. Stir in cubed cooked chicken, chicken broth, and tomato paste. Bring to boiling.

Stir together sour cream and flour. Stir into mixture in skillet. Cook and stir till thickened and bubbly. Cook and stir for 1 minute more. Serve chicken mixture over noodles. If desired, garnish with parsley sprig. Makes 4 servings.

*Nutrition information per serving: 542 calories, 32 g protein, 33 g carbohydrate, 31 g fat (11 g saturated), 119 mg cholesterol, 592 mg sodium.*

# Pacific Rim Stir-Fry

*Adjust the hotness of this stir-fry by reducing or increasing the amount of chili oil used.*

3 ounces rice sticks (also called rice noodles) or packaged dried vermicelli, broken

12 ounces skinless, boneless chicken thighs or breast halves

½ cup chicken broth

2 tablespoons snipped fresh basil or 2 teaspoons dried basil, crushed

2 tablespoons soy sauce

2 teaspoons cornstarch

1 teaspoon chili oil or ½ teaspoon crushed red pepper

½ teaspoon ground turmeric

1 tablespoon cooking oil

2 medium carrots, cut into julienne strips

2 cups broccoli flowerets

1 red or green sweet pepper, cut into lengthwise strips

¼ cup cashew halves or peanuts

In a saucepan cook rice sticks in boiling water for 3 minutes. (Or, cook vermicelli according to package directions.) Drain; keep warm.

Meanwhile, rinse chicken; pat dry with paper towels. Cut chicken thighs or breasts into thin, bite-size strips; set aside.

For sauce, in a small bowl combine chicken broth, basil, soy sauce, cornstarch, chili oil or crushed red pepper, and turmeric; set aside.

Add cooking oil to a wok or 12-inch skillet. Preheat over medium-high heat (add more oil if necessary during cooking). Stir-fry carrot strips in hot oil for 1 minute. Add broccoli; stir-fry for 2 minutes more. Add sweet pepper strips; stir-fry for 1½ to 3 minutes more or till crisp-tender. Remove from wok. Add the chicken to wok; stir-fry for 2 to 3 minutes or till tender and no longer pink. Push from center of wok.

Stir sauce; add to center of wok. Cook and stir till thickened and bubbly. Return cooked vegetables to wok. Stir to coat. Cook and stir about 2 minutes more or till heated through. Serve immediately over hot rice sticks or vermicelli. Top with cashews or peanuts. Makes 4 servings.

*Nutrition information per serving: 309 calories, 17 g protein, 32 g carbohydrate, 13 g fat (3 g saturated), 41 mg cholesterol, 748 mg sodium.*

# Chicken-Mushroom Lo Mein

*Enjoy lo mein at home without calling the Chinese take-out—it's easy and tastes terrific.*

12  ounces skinless, boneless chicken
    breast halves or thighs
2   tablespoons soy sauce
2   tablespoons dry sherry
2   teaspoons cornstarch
8   ounces packaged dried linguine
1   tablespoon cooking oil
1   tablespoon toasted sesame oil
8   ounces fresh mushrooms, sliced
1   medium red or green sweet pepper,
    cut into 2-inch strips
4   green onions, cut into 2-inch pieces
6   ounces fresh pea pods, strings
    removed (1½ cups)
½   cup water
¼   teaspoon instant chicken bouillon
    granules

Rinse chicken; pat dry with paper towels. Cut chicken into thin, bite-size strips. For marinade, in a small bowl stir together soy sauce, dry sherry, and cornstarch. Add chicken; stir to coat. Cover and chill for 30 minutes.

Meanwhile, cook the pasta according to package directions, omitting oil and salt. Drain well.

Add cooking oil and sesame oil to a wok or 12-inch skillet. Preheat over medium-high heat (add more oil if necessary during cooking). Stir-fry mushrooms, sweet pepper, and green onions in hot oil for 2 minutes. Add pea pods; stir-fry about 1 minute more or till vegetables are crisp-tender. Remove from wok.

Drain chicken, reserving marinade. Stir-fry chicken for 2 to 3 minutes or till tender and no longer pink. Push from center of wok. Combine water, bouillon granules, and marinade; add to center of wok. Cook and stir till thickened and bubbly. Add the pasta and cooked vegetables. Stir to coat. Cook and stir about 1 minute more or till heated through. Makes 4 servings.

*Nutrition information per serving: 434 calories, 28 g protein, 54 g carbohydrate, 11 g fat (2 g saturated), 45 mg cholesterol, 616 mg sodium.*

# Broccoli Chicken Stir-Fry

*Using shredded lettuce instead of rice adds a pleasant crispness and lightness to this stir-fry.*

12  ounces skinless, boneless chicken
    breast halves
1   pound broccoli
½   cup chicken broth
2   tablespoons teriyaki sauce
2   teaspoons cornstarch
1   teaspoon toasted sesame oil
2   tablespoons cooking oil
1   tablespoon grated gingerroot
1   clove garlic, minced
2   cups fresh medium mushrooms,
    halved or quartered
8   ounces fresh bean sprouts (2 cups)
1   red or green sweet pepper, cut into
    lengthwise strips
1   8-ounce can sliced water chestnuts,
    drained
4   cups coarsely shredded lettuce
    (optional)

Rinse chicken; pat dry with paper towels. Cut chicken into 1-inch pieces. Remove flowerets from broccoli and cut in half (you should have about 3½ cups). Cut stalks into 1½-inch lengths and then into ¼-inch strips (you should have about 1½ cups). Set aside.

For sauce, in a small bowl combine chicken broth, teriyaki sauce, cornstarch, and sesame oil; set aside.

Add cooking oil to a wok or 12-inch skillet. Preheat over medium-high heat (add more oil if necessary during cooking). Stir-fry gingerroot and garlic in hot oil for 10 seconds. Add the broccoli stems; stir-fry for 1 minute. Add broccoli flowerets; stir-fry for 2 to 3 minutes or till crisp-tender. Remove broccoli.

Add mushrooms to wok; stir-fry about 1½ minutes or till crisp-tender. Remove from wok. Add bean sprouts and sweet pepper to wok; stir-fry for 1 to 2 minutes or till crisp-tender. Remove from wok. Add chicken to wok. Stir-fry for 3 to 4 minutes or till tender and no longer pink. Push chicken from center of wok.

Stir sauce; add to center of wok. Cook and stir till thickened and bubbly. Return cooked vegetables to wok. Add water chestnuts. Stir to coat. Cook and stir about 2 minutes more or till heated through. If desired, spoon chicken mixture over lettuce. Serve immediately. Makes 4 servings.

*Nutrition information per serving: 261 calories, 24 g protein, 19 g carbohydrate, 11 g fat (2 g saturated), 45 mg cholesterol, 524 mg sodium.*

# Cincinnati-Style Chicken Chili

*Add a sprinkling of freshly shredded Romano cheese to boost the flavor of this Midwestern favorite.*

1  pound ground raw chicken
1  large onion, chopped
1  clove garlic, minced
3  tablespoons chili powder
2  teaspoons paprika
1  teaspoon ground cumin
½  teaspoon salt
½  teaspoon ground cinnamon
⅛  teaspoon ground cloves
⅛  teaspoon ground red pepper
1  bay leaf
1  14½-ounce can stewed tomatoes
1  8-ounce can tomato sauce
½  cup water
1  tablespoon red wine vinegar
1  tablespoon molasses
1  15½-ounce can red kidney beans
   Hot cooked spaghetti

In a 4½-quart Dutch oven cook ground chicken, onion, and garlic over medium heat for 5 to 7 minutes or till chicken is no longer pink. Drain fat, if necessary.

Add chili powder, paprika, cumin, salt, cinnamon, cloves, red pepper, and bay leaf. Cook and stir over medium heat for 3 minutes more.

Stir in undrained stewed tomatoes, tomato sauce, water, red wine vinegar, and molasses. Bring to boiling; reduce heat. Cover and simmer for 45 minutes, stirring occasionally.

Uncover and simmer to desired consistency. Discard bay leaf. In a medium saucepan heat undrained kidney beans; drain. To serve, spoon the chicken mixture and beans over cooked spaghetti. Makes 4 servings.

*Nutrition information per serving: 402 calories, 30 g protein, 61 g carbohydrate, 8 g fat (2 g saturated), 54 mg cholesterol, 1,223 mg sodium.*

## Serving Cincinnati-Style

Visit Cincinnati and you can sample chili that's unlike any you'll find in Texas or the Southwest. Cincinnati natives love their chili served over spaghetti or other pasta. What's more, they often sprinkle it with shredded cheese, chopped onion, and other toppers.

# Chicken Vegetable Ragout

*Mop up the thick, well-seasoned sauce with some crusty French bread.*

2   pounds meaty chicken pieces
        (breasts, thighs, and drumsticks)
2   tablespoons cooking oil
8   ounces fresh mushrooms, quartered
1   large onion, chopped (1 cup)
2   cloves garlic, minced
1   bay leaf
1   tablespoon snipped fresh thyme or
        1 teaspoon dried thyme, crushed
½   teaspoon pepper
¼   teaspoon salt
2   cups chicken broth
½   cup dry white wine
4   medium carrots, cut into 1½-inch
        chunks
4   parsnips, peeled and cut into
        1½-inch chunks
⅓   cup chicken broth
3   tablespoons all-purpose flour
    Snipped parsley (optional)

Skin chicken. Rinse chicken; pat dry with paper towels. In a 4½-quart Dutch oven cook chicken in hot oil over medium heat about 15 minutes or till lightly browned, turning to brown evenly. Remove chicken.

Add the mushrooms, onion, garlic, bay leaf, thyme, pepper, and salt to Dutch oven. Cook for 4 to 5 minutes or till vegetables are tender. Carefully stir in 2 cups chicken broth and the white wine. Add carrots and parsnips. Return chicken to Dutch oven. Bring to boiling; reduce heat. Cover and simmer for 35 to 40 minutes or till chicken is tender and no longer pink and vegetables are tender.

Using a slotted spoon, transfer chicken and vegetables to a serving dish; keep warm. If necessary, spoon excess fat from broth mixture. Discard bay leaf. In a small bowl combine ⅓ cup chicken broth and the flour. Stir into broth mixture. Cook and stir till thickened and bubbly. Cook and stir for 1 minute more. Spoon sauce over chicken and vegetables. If desired, garnish with parsley. Makes 4 servings.

*Nutrition information per serving: 466 calories, 40 g protein, 32 g carbohydrate, 18 g fat (4 g saturated), 104 mg cholesterol, 769 mg sodium.*

# Chicken with Apricots and Prunes

*Boost the flavor in the rice accompaniment with toasted slivered almonds and snipped parsley.*

2  to 2½ pounds meaty chicken pieces
       (breasts, thighs, and drumsticks)
½  teaspoon salt
½  teaspoon garlic powder
¼  teaspoon pepper
2  tablespoons cooking oil
1  6-ounce package dried apricots
1  cup pitted prunes, cut into halves
1  cup chicken broth
¾  cup dry white wine
¼  cup white wine vinegar
1  tablespoon brown sugar
3  inches stick cinnamon
4  whole cloves
3  tablespoons Dijon-style mustard
3  tablespoons water
4  teaspoons all-purpose flour
    Hot cooked rice
    Thinly sliced green onion (optional)

If desired, skin chicken. Rinse chicken; pat dry with paper towels. Sprinkle chicken with salt, garlic powder, and pepper. In a 4½-quart Dutch oven cook chicken in hot oil over medium heat about 15 minutes or till lightly browned, turning to brown evenly. Drain fat.

Add apricots, prunes, broth, white wine, wine vinegar, brown sugar, cinnamon, and cloves. Bring to boiling; reduce heat. Cover and simmer for 35 to 40 minutes or till chicken is tender and no longer pink.

Using a slotted spoon, transfer chicken and fruit to a platter; keep warm. Discard cinnamon and cloves. For sauce, in a small bowl stir together the mustard, water, and flour. Stir into broth mixture. Cook and stir till thickened and bubbly. Cook and stir for 1 minute more. Serve chicken and fruit over cooked rice. Top with some of the sauce. If desired, garnish with green onion. Pass remaining sauce. Makes 6 servings.

*Nutrition information per serving: 570 calories, 29 g protein, 82 g carbohydrate, 13 g fat (3 g saturated), 69 mg cholesterol, 580 mg sodium.*

# Spinach Fettuccine with Chicken

*Although packaged grated Parmesan can be used here, we find that freshly grated or shredded cheese intensifies the flavor. If you use a food processor, you'll have all the cheese you'll need in no time.*

6 ounces packaged dried spinach or plain fettuccine
4 ounces fresh mushrooms, sliced
¼ cup sliced green onions
2 tablespoons margarine or butter
2 tablespoons all-purpose flour
¼ teaspoon salt
¼ teaspoon coarsely ground pepper
¼ teaspoon ground nutmeg
1½ cups milk
½ cup grated or finely shredded Parmesan cheese
2 tablespoons dry sherry
2 cups cubed cooked chicken (10 ounces)
½ cup sliced pitted ripe olives
Snipped chives (optional)
Lemon wedges (optional)

Cook fettuccine according to package directions. Drain well. Meanwhile, in a 12-inch skillet cook mushrooms and green onions in the margarine or butter about 5 minutes or till vegetables are tender. Stir in flour, salt, pepper, and nutmeg. Add milk all at once. Cook and stir till thickened and bubbly. Cook and stir for 1 minute more. Add half of the Parmesan cheese and the sherry; cook and stir till cheese is melted.

Add the cooked fettuccine, chicken, and ripe olives to vegetable mixture. Toss lightly to coat. Sprinkle with the remaining Parmesan cheese and, if desired, chives. If desired, garnish with lemon. Makes 4 servings.

*Nutrition information per serving: 506 calories, 37 g protein, 42 g carbohydrate, 20 g fat (7 g saturated), 84 mg cholesterol, 639 mg sodium.*

# Hearty Chicken and Noodles

*In this hearty dish, chicken legs turn rather ordinary vegetables into a comforting home-style dinner.*

3 chicken legs (thigh-drumstick pieces) (about 2 pounds total)
4 cups water
½ cup chopped celery leaves
2 tablespoons snipped parsley
1 bay leaf
1 teaspoon dried thyme, crushed
1 teaspoon salt
¼ teaspoon pepper
2 cups sliced carrots
1½ cups chopped onion
1 cup sliced celery
3 cups packaged dried wide noodles
2 cups milk
1 cup loose-pack frozen peas
2 tablespoons all-purpose flour

Skin chicken. Rinse chicken; pat dry. In a 4½-quart Dutch oven place chicken, water, celery leaves, parsley, bay leaf, thyme, salt, and pepper. Bring to boiling; reduce heat. Cover and simmer for 30 minutes. Add carrots, onion, and sliced celery. Cover and simmer about 30 minutes more or till chicken is tender and no longer pink. Remove from heat. Remove chicken; cool slightly. Remove meat from bones; discard bones. Chop chicken and set aside. Discard bay leaf.

Bring vegetable mixture to boiling. Add noodles; cook for 5 minutes. Stir in 1½ cups of the milk and the peas. In a screw-top jar combine remaining milk and flour. Cover and shake till smooth. Stir into noodle mixture. Cook and stir till thickened and bubbly. Stir in the chicken. Cook for 1 to 2 minutes more or till heated through. Makes 6 servings.

*Nutrition information per serving: 321 calories, 24 g protein, 38 g carbohydrate, 8 g fat (2 g saturated), 83 mg cholesterol, 535 mg sodium.*

# Oven-Fried Chicken

*Accompany with sliced tomatoes sprinkled with basil and marinated in a light salad dressing.*

| | |
|---|---|
| 1 | **beaten egg** |
| 3 | **tablespoons milk** |
| 1 | **cup finely crushed saltine crackers (about 28)** |
| 1 | **teaspoon dried thyme, crushed** |
| ½ | **teaspoon paprika** |
| ⅛ | **teaspoon pepper** |
| 2½ | **to 3 pounds meaty chicken pieces (breasts, thighs, and drumsticks)** |
| 2 | **tablespoons margarine or butter, melted** |

In a small bowl combine the egg and the milk. In a shallow dish combine the crackers, thyme, paprika, and pepper. Set aside.

Skin chicken. Rinse chicken; pat dry with paper towels. Dip chicken pieces, one at a time, in egg mixture, then roll in cracker mixture.

In a greased 15x10x1-inch or 13x9x2-inch baking pan arrange chicken so the pieces don't touch. Drizzle chicken pieces with melted margarine or butter.

Bake in a 375° oven for 45 to 55 minutes or till the chicken pieces are tender and no longer pink. Do not turn the chicken pieces while baking. Makes 6 servings.

*Nutrition information per serving: 253 calories, 24 g protein, 10 g carbohydrate, 12 g fat (3 g saturated), 105 mg cholesterol, 296 mg sodium.*

# Honeyed Chicken

*For a zippy appetizer, use this glaze for 10 to 12 chicken wings (cut the wings at the joints and discard tips).*

| | |
|---|---|
| 8 | **chicken drumsticks and/or thighs (about 2 pounds total)** |
| ¼ | **cup finely chopped green onions** |
| ¼ | **cup honey** |
| ¼ | **teaspoon garlic powder** |
| | **Dash ground red pepper** |

Rinse chicken; pat dry with paper towels. Arrange in a 15x10x1-inch baking pan so the pieces don't touch. Bake in a 400° oven for 30 minutes.

Meanwhile, combine the green onions, honey, garlic powder, and ground red pepper. Brush over chicken. Bake for 15 to 20 minutes more or till golden brown and chicken is no longer pink. Makes 4 servings.

*Nutrition information per serving: 327 calories, 29 g protein, 17 g carbohydrate, 15 g fat (4 g saturated), 103 mg cholesterol, 98 mg sodium.*

# Blue Cheese-Stuffed Chicken Breasts

*Complete the meal with steamed carrots sprinkled with parsley and a refreshing lemon sherbet for the finale.*

4   medium skinless, boneless chicken
      breast halves (about 1 pound total)
    Salt
    Pepper
½   cup chopped pecans, toasted
1   3-ounce package cream cheese,
      softened
¼   cup crumbled blue cheese (1 ounce)
2   tablespoons margarine or butter,
      melted
¼   teaspoon paprika

Rinse chicken; pat dry with paper towels. Place each half between 2 pieces of plastic wrap. Working from center to edges, pound lightly with the flat side of a meat mallet to ¼-inch thickness. Remove plastic wrap. Sprinkle with salt and pepper.

In a small bowl combine pecans, cream cheese, and blue cheese. Place about ¼ cup cheese mixture on each chicken piece. Fold in the sides; roll up jelly-roll style, pressing edges to seal.

Place chicken in a 2-quart square baking dish. In a small bowl combine margarine or butter and paprika. Brush chicken with mixture. Bake, uncovered, in a 350° oven about 30 minutes or till chicken is tender and no longer pink. Makes 4 servings.

*Nutrition information per serving: 363 calories, 26 g protein, 4 g carbohydrate, 28 g fat (9 g saturated), 88 mg cholesterol, 417 mg sodium.*

# Chicken with Saffron Rice

*Here's a simple version of a Spanish paella traditionally named after the utensil it's cooked in— a two-handled pan that also serves as a casserole.*

6   large chicken breast halves or
      thighs (about 2 pounds total)
2   tablespoons cooking oil
1   medium onion, chopped (½ cup)
2   cloves garlic, minced
1   cup long grain rice
1   6½-ounce can minced clams
1   teaspoon ground cumin
½   teaspoon salt
¼   teaspoon pepper
⅛   teaspoon ground saffron or
      ¼ teaspoon thread saffron
1   14½-ounce can stewed tomatoes
1   14½-ounce can chicken broth
¼   cup water
1   10-ounce package frozen peas
8   ounces medium raw shrimp, shelled
      and deveined
½   cup sliced pitted ripe olives
      Parsley sprigs (optional)

Rinse chicken; pat dry with paper towels. In a 12-inch ovenproof skillet cook chicken in hot oil over medium heat about 10 minutes or till chicken is lightly browned, turning to brown evenly. Remove chicken.

Add onion and garlic to skillet. Cook about 5 minutes or till onion is tender. Stir in rice. Cook and stir till rice is light brown.

Drain clams, reserving liquid; set aside. Stir cumin, salt, pepper, and saffron into rice mixture. Stir in undrained tomatoes, chicken broth, water, and reserved clam liquid. Bring to boiling. Top with chicken pieces. Cover tightly and bake in a 400° oven for 15 minutes.

Stir in reserved clams, peas, shrimp, and olives. Cover and bake about 15 minutes more or till chicken is tender and no longer pink and shrimp turn pink. Let stand for 5 minutes before serving. If desired, garnish with parsley. Makes 6 servings.

*Nutrition information per serving: 437 calories, 41 g protein, 42 g carbohydrate, 12 g fat (3 g saturated), 145 mg cholesterol, 893 mg sodium.*

## Savoring Saffron

Saffron is the world's most expensive spice because its filaments must be carefully picked by hand. If you're using saffron threads, release the wonderful flavor by rubbing the threads between your fingers before adding them to the other ingredients.

# Herbed Chicken With Spinach Stuffing

*Serve wedges of roasted white or sweet potatoes on the side.*

1   5- to 6-pound whole roasting chicken
1   tablespoon olive oil or cooking oil
1   teaspoon dried basil, crushed
1   teaspoon dried oregano, crushed
1   teaspoon dried parsley flakes
¼   teaspoon garlic salt
2   10-ounce packages frozen chopped spinach, thawed and well drained
1   cup chopped red sweet pepper
4   ounces fully cooked ham, chopped
¾   cup soft bread crumbs (1 slice)
½   cup sliced green onions
⅓   cup pine nuts or slivered almonds
¼   cup margarine or butter, melted
¼   teaspoon black pepper
    Green onion fans (optional)
    Red sweet pepper pieces (optional)

Rinse chicken; pat dry with paper towels. Brush with oil. In a small bowl combine basil, oregano, parsley, and garlic salt. Sprinkle over chicken; rub in with your fingers. Cover and chill for up to 24 hours.

For stuffing, combine the spinach, chopped red sweet pepper, ham, bread crumbs, sliced green onions, nuts, margarine or butter, and black pepper. If desired, cover and chill up to 24 hours.

Slip your fingers between the skin and breast meat of the bird, forming a pocket. Spoon some of stuffing into pocket. Spoon some of the stuffing loosely into the neck cavity. Pull neck skin to back; fasten with a small skewer. Lightly spoon the remaining stuffing into the body cavity. Tuck drumsticks under the band of skin that crosses the tail. If there is no band, tie drumsticks to the tail. Twist the wing tips under the chicken.

Place stuffed chicken, breast side up, on a rack in a shallow roasting pan. Insert a meat thermometer into the center of an inside thigh muscle. The bulb should not touch the bone. Roast, uncovered, in a 325° oven for 1¾ to 2½ hours or till meat thermometer registers 180° to 185°. At this time, chicken is no longer pink and the drumsticks move easily in their sockets. When two-thirds done, cut band of skin or string between drumsticks so thighs will cook evenly. Remove from oven; cover with foil. Let stand for 10 to 20 minutes before carving. If desired, garnish with green onion fans and red pepper pieces. Makes 10 servings.

*Nutrition information per serving: 514 calories, 38 g protein, 7 g carbohydrate, 38 g fat (8 g saturated), 93 mg cholesterol, 586 mg sodium.*

# Fruit-Stuffed Roasted Chicken

*While the bird roasts to perfection, tuck some rice pudding in the oven to bake alongside.*

1 5- to 6-pound whole roasting
   chicken
   Salt
   Pepper
¼ cup margarine or butter, melted
¼ cup dry sherry
4½ teaspoons snipped fresh thyme or
     1½ teaspoons dried thyme,
     crushed
2 teaspoons finely shredded orange
   peel
2 medium apples, cored and chopped
   (2 cups)
1 medium onion, chopped (½ cup)
½ cup chopped celery
2 cups cubed French bread (¾-inch
   cubes)
10 pitted prunes or dried apricots,
    cut up
1 cup seedless green grapes, halved
2 tablespoons orange juice

Rinse chicken; pat dry. Sprinkle body cavity with salt and pepper. In a small bowl combine 2 tablespoons melted margarine, 2 tablespoons sherry, 1 tablespoon fresh thyme or 1 teaspoon dried thyme, and 1 teaspoon orange peel. Brush chicken with sherry mixture.

For stuffing, in a medium skillet cook apples, onion, and celery in the remaining melted margarine about 5 minutes or till tender. In a large bowl combine apple mixture, French bread, prunes or apricots, grapes, orange juice, remaining dry sherry, remaining fresh or dried thyme, and remaining orange peel. (Stuffing will become more moist while cooking.) Spoon some of the stuffing loosely into the neck cavity. Pull neck skin to back; fasten with a small skewer. Lightly spoon the remaining stuffing into body cavity. Tuck drumsticks under the band of skin that crosses the tail. If there is no band, tie drumsticks to the tail. Twist the wing tips under the chicken.

Place stuffed chicken, breast side up, on a rack in a shallow roasting pan. Insert a meat thermometer into the center of an inside thigh muscle. The bulb should not touch the bone. Roast, uncovered, in a 325° oven for 1¾ to 2½ hours or till meat thermometer registers 180° to 185°. At this time, chicken is no longer pink and the drumsticks move easily in their sockets. When the bird is two-thirds done, cut the band of skin or string between drumsticks so thighs will cook evenly.

Remove from oven; cover with foil. Let stand for 10 to 20 minutes before carving. Makes 10 servings.

*Nutrition information per serving: 393 calories, 33 g protein, 22 g carbohydrate, 18 g fat (5 g saturated), 93 mg cholesterol, 250 mg sodium.*

# Roasted Chicken with Cherry Sauce

*You can skip the brandy in the cherry sauce if you wish--just add a little more apple juice.*

| | |
|---|---|
| 1 | **5- to 6-pound whole roasting chicken** |
| 1 | **tablespoon olive oil or cooking oil** |
| ½ | **teaspoon garlic powder** |
| ½ | **teaspoon dried tarragon, crushed** |
| ¼ | **teaspoon salt** |
| ¼ | **teaspoon pepper** |
| ½ | **of a medium lemon, sliced** |
| 1 | **sprig parsley** |
| 3 | **tablespoons brown sugar** |
| 4 | **teaspoons cornstarch** |
| 2 | **cups frozen tart red cherries** |
| ¾ | **cup apple juice** |
| 1 | **tablespoon lemon juice** |
| 2 | **tablespoons brandy** |

Rinse chicken; pat dry with paper towels. Brush with oil. In a small bowl combine garlic powder, tarragon, salt, and pepper. Sprinkle over chicken; rub in with your fingers. Place lemon slices and parsley in body cavity. Tuck the drumsticks under the band of skin that crosses the tail. If there is no band, tie drumsticks to the tail. Twist the wing tips under the chicken.

Place chicken, breast side up, on a rack in a shallow roasting pan. Insert a meat thermometer into the center of an inside thigh muscle. The bulb should not touch the bone. Roast, uncovered, in a 325° oven for 1¾ to 2½ hours or till meat thermometer registers 180° to 185°. At this time, chicken is no longer pink and the drumsticks move easily in their sockets. When the bird is two-thirds done, cut the band of skin or string between drumsticks so thighs will cook evenly. Remove chicken from oven; cover with foil. Let stand for 10 to 20 minutes before carving.

Meanwhile, for sauce, in a medium saucepan stir together the brown sugar and cornstarch. Stir in the cherries, apple juice, and lemon juice. Cook and stir till thickened and bubbly. Cook and stir for 2 minutes more. Stir in brandy. Heat through. Serve sauce with chicken. Makes 10 servings.

*Nutrition information per serving: 304 calories, 32 g protein, 11 g carbohydrate, 14 g fat (4 g saturated), 93 mg cholesterol, 212 mg sodium.*

# Minnesota Apple- and Wild Rice-Stuffed Chicken

*Team up this bird with a chicory and red onion salad dressed with a blue cheese vinaigrette.*

1  6-ounce package long grain and wild rice mix
8  ounces sliced fresh mushrooms (3 cups)
2  medium cooking apples (such as Granny Smith or Jonathan), cored and chopped
1  cup shredded carrot
½  cup thinly sliced green onions
½  teaspoon pepper
1  5- to 6-pound whole roasting chicken
2  to 3 tablespoons apple jelly, melted
   Apple wedges (optional)

For stuffing, cook rice according to package directions, except add mushrooms, apples, carrot, green onions, and pepper to rice before cooking.

Meanwhile, rinse chicken; pat dry with paper towels. Spoon some of the stuffing loosely into neck cavity. Pull neck skin to back; fasten with a small skewer. Lightly spoon the remaining stuffing into body cavity. Tuck drumsticks under the band of skin that crosses the tail. If there is no band, tie drumsticks to tail. Twist the wing tips under the chicken.

Place stuffed chicken, breast side up, on a rack in a shallow roasting pan. Insert meat thermometer into the center of an inside thigh muscle. The bulb should not touch the bone. Roast, uncovered, in a 325° oven for 1¾ to 2½ hours or till meat thermometer registers 180° to 185°. At this time, chicken is no longer pink and the drumsticks move easily in their sockets. When the bird is two-thirds done, cut the band of skin or string between drumsticks so thighs will cook evenly. Brush chicken with melted jelly once or twice during the last 10 minutes of roasting.

Remove chicken from oven; cover with foil. Let stand for 10 to 20 minutes before carving. Transfer chicken to a serving platter. Spoon some of the stuffing around the chicken. If desired, garnish with apple wedges. Makes 10 servings.

*Nutrition information per serving: 332 calories, 34 g protein, 19 g carbohydrate, 13 g fat (4 g saturated), 93 mg cholesterol, 365 mg sodium.*

# All-American Barbecued Chicken

*Make it an All-American barbecue with roasted corn on the cob and macaroni salad.*

1   medium onion, finely chopped
    (½ cup)
1   tablespoon cooking oil
1   cup catsup
½   cup water
¼   cup vinegar
2   to 3 tablespoons brown sugar
2   tablespoons Worcestershire sauce
2   dashes bottled hot pepper sauce
1   2½- to 3-pound broiler-fryer
    chicken, quartered

For sauce, cook onion in hot oil till tender. Stir in the catsup, water, vinegar, sugar, Worcestershire, and pepper sauce. Bring to boiling; reduce heat. Simmer, uncovered, about 15 minutes or to desired consistency.

Meanwhile, rinse chicken; pat dry with paper towels. Break wing, hip, and drumstick joints so pieces lie flat. Twist wing tips under back. Grill chicken, skin side down, on an uncovered grill directly over medium coals for 35 to 40 minutes or till chicken is tender and no longer pink, turning once. Brush with sauce during the last 10 minutes of grilling. Heat remaining sauce till bubbly; pass with chicken. Makes 4 to 6 servings.

*Nutrition information per serving: 407 calories, 32 g protein, 29 g carbohydrate, 19 g fat (5 g saturated), 98 mg cholesterol, 996 mg sodium.*

# Barbecued Chicken Thighs

*Grill chunks of red sweet pepper, corn on the cob, and zucchini on skewers for a quick serve-along.*

3   tablespoons brown sugar
2   tablespoons finely chopped onion
2   tablespoons vinegar
2   tablespoons prepared mustard
¼   teaspoon celery seed
⅛   teaspoon garlic powder
8   chicken thighs (about 2½ pounds
    total)
½   teaspoon paprika
¼   teaspoon salt
¼   teaspoon ground turmeric

For sauce, combine the brown sugar, onion, vinegar, mustard, celery seed, and garlic powder. Bring to boiling, stirring till sugar dissolves. Remove from heat.

If desired, skin chicken. Rinse chicken; pat dry. Combine paprika, salt, and turmeric; rub over chicken. Grill chicken on an uncovered grill directly over medium coals for 35 to 40 minutes or till tender and no longer pink, turning once. Brush with sauce during the last 5 minutes of grilling. Makes 4 servings.

*Nutrition information per serving: 375 calories, 37 g protein, 11 g carbohydrate, 19 g fat (5 g saturated), 129 mg cholesterol, 366 mg sodium.*

# Chicken Fajitas with Guacamole

*You can make this chunky guacamole up to 4 hours before serving. Just keep it covered and refrigerated so it won't darken.*

¼ cup olive oil or cooking oil
¼ cup snipped cilantro or parsley
1 teaspoon finely shredded lemon peel
2 tablespoons lemon juice
1 teaspoon chili powder
½ teaspoon ground cumin
½ teaspoon pepper
12 ounces skinless, boneless chicken breast halves
8 8-inch flour tortillas
2 cups shredded lettuce
1 cup shredded cheddar cheese (4 ounces)
1 large tomato, chopped
½ cup sliced pitted ripe olives
Guacamole

For marinade, in a shallow nonmetallic dish combine oil, cilantro or parsley, lemon peel, lemon juice, chili powder, cumin, and pepper. Rinse chicken; pat dry with paper towels. Add chicken to marinade, turning to coat. Cover and chill about 1 hour.

Drain chicken, reserving marinade. Grill chicken on an uncovered grill directly over medium coals for 12 to 15 minutes or till chicken is tender and no longer pink, turning and brushing once with marinade. (Or, place chicken on the unheated rack of a broiler pan. Broil 5 to 6 inches from the heat for 10 to 12 minutes, turning and brushing once with marinade.) Wrap flour tortillas in foil; heat on grill or in oven during the last 5 minutes of cooking chicken.

To serve, cut chicken into bite-size strips. On each tortilla, arrange chicken strips, lettuce, cheese, tomato, and olives. Roll up tortillas, tucking in sides. Serve with Guacamole. Makes 4 servings.

**Guacamole:** Seed and peel 1 ripe *avocado*. In a mixing bowl coarsely mash avocado. Stir in 1 medium *tomato,* seeded, chopped, and drained; 2 tablespoons finely chopped *onion;* 1 tablespoon *lemon juice;* and ¼ teaspoon *salt.* Cover the surface of the guacamole with plastic wrap and chill up to 4 hours.

*Nutrition information per serving: 576 calories, 30 g protein, 45 g carbohydrate, 32 g fat (10 g saturated), 74 mg cholesterol, 745 mg sodium.*

# Texas-Style Barbecued Chicken Legs

*Cut lengthwise strips of assorted sweet peppers and grill to perfection alongside the chicken.*

1   medium onion, finely chopped
      (½ cup)
2   cloves garlic, minced
1   teaspoon chili powder
¼   teaspoon ground sage
1   tablespoon margarine or butter
½   cup catsup
2   tablespoons water
2   tablespoons vinegar
1   tablespoon sugar
1   tablespoon lemon juice
1   tablespoon Worcestershire sauce
½   teaspoon salt
½   teaspoon bottled hot pepper sauce
¼   teaspoon cracked black pepper
6   chicken legs (thigh-drumstick
      pieces) (3 to 3½ pounds total)

For sauce, in a small saucepan cook onion, garlic, chili powder, and sage in margarine or butter till onion is tender. Stir in catsup, water, vinegar, sugar, lemon juice, Worcestershire sauce, salt, hot pepper sauce, and black pepper. Bring to boiling; reduce heat. Simmer, uncovered, for 5 minutes, stirring occasionally.

Meanwhile, rinse chicken; pat dry with paper towels. Grill chicken, skin side down, on an uncovered grill directly over medium coals for 35 to 40 minutes or till chicken is tender and no longer pink, turning once. (Or, place chicken on the unheated rack of a broiler pan. Broil 5 to 6 inches from the heat for 28 to 32 minutes, turning once.) Brush with sauce during the last 10 minutes of grilling or broiling.

Heat the remaining sauce till bubbly; pass with chicken. Makes 6 servings.

*Nutrition information per serving: 276 calories, 25 g protein, 11 g carbohydrate, 15 g fat (4 g saturated), 86 mg cholesterol, 596 mg sodium.*

## Chopped Onions the Easy Way

To chop onions quickly, first cut the onion in half. Use the cut side as a base to stabilize the piece. Slice the onion half in one direction; holding the slices together with one hand, slice in the other direction. The job is easier if you use a chef's knife because it's designed to let you grasp the handle without your fingers touching the cutting surface.

# Grilled Chicken with Peach Salsa

*This brightly colored peach salsa adds a flavor burst and a southwestern feel to the wine-marinated chicken.*

4   chicken legs (thigh-drumstick
        pieces) (2 to 2½ pounds total)
        Wine Marinade
2   medium peaches or nectarines or
        1⅓ cups frozen unsweetened
        peach slices, thawed
½   cup chopped red sweet pepper
½   of a ripe avocado, seeded, peeled,
        and finely chopped
2   green onions, finely chopped
½   teaspoon finely shredded lime peel
2   tablespoons lime juice
1   tablespoon snipped cilantro
        Red sweet pepper cutouts (optional)

Rinse chicken; pat dry with paper towels. Add chicken to Wine Marinade, turning to coat. Cover and chill about 1 hour.

Meanwhile, for salsa, peel and pit the fresh peaches or pit the nectarines. Finely chop peaches or nectarines. In a bowl combine the peaches or nectarines, chopped red pepper, avocado, green onions, lime peel, lime juice, and cilantro. Cover and chill till serving time.

Drain chicken, reserving marinade. Grill chicken, skin side down, on an uncovered grill directly over medium coals for 35 to 40 minutes or till chicken is tender and no longer pink, turning once. (Or, place chicken on the unheated rack of a broiler pan. Broil 5 to 6 inches from the heat for 28 to 32 minutes, turning once.) Brush with marinade up to the last 5 minutes of grilling or broiling. Serve chicken with salsa. If desired, garnish with red pepper cutouts. Makes 4 servings.

**Wine Marinade:** In a shallow nonmetallic dish combine ½ cup *dry white wine;* 1½ teaspoons finely shredded *orange peel;* ⅓ cup *orange juice;* 2 tablespoons *olive oil* or *cooking oil;* 1½ teaspoons snipped *fresh rosemary* or ½ teaspoon *dried rosemary,* crushed; and 1 *bay leaf.*

*Nutrition information per serving: 311 calories, 25 g protein, 5 g carbohydrate, 20 g fat (4 g saturated), 86 mg cholesterol, 85 mg sodium.*

# Skewered Chicken with Papaya Chutney

*Accompany these chicken kabobs with steamed rice spiked with dried crushed red pepper.*

1 medium onion, cut into 8 wedges
1 tablespoon curry powder
2 tablespoons olive oil or cooking oil
2 tablespoons lemon juice
1 tablespoon water
½ teaspoon salt
¼ teaspoon pepper
1 pound skinless, boneless chicken breast halves or thighs
1 red or green sweet pepper, cut into 1-inch pieces
12 fresh or canned pineapple chunks
Papaya Chutney

In a small saucepan cook the onion in boiling water for 4 minutes. Drain; set aside. Meanwhile, in a small skillet cook curry powder in hot oil for 30 seconds. Remove from heat. Stir in lemon juice, water, salt, and pepper; set aside.

Rinse chicken; pat dry with paper towels. Cut chicken into 1-inch cubes. On 4 long metal skewers thread chicken cubes, sweet pepper, pineapple, and onion. Stir curry mixture; brush kabobs on all sides. Grill kabobs on an uncovered grill directly over medium coals for 12 to 14 minutes or till chicken is tender and no longer pink, turning to brown evenly. (Or, place kabobs on the unheated rack of a broiler pan. Broil 5 to 6 inches from the heat for 10 to 12 minutes, turning to brown evenly.) Serve with Papaya Chutney. Makes 4 servings.

**Papaya Chutney:** In a medium saucepan combine 1 cup chopped, peeled *apple*; 1 cup chopped, peeled *papaya*; ¼ cup packed *brown sugar*; 2 tablespoons *raisins*; 2 tablespoons chopped *green sweet pepper*; 2 tablespoons *vinegar*; 2 tablespoons *water*; 2 teaspoons *lemon juice*; and dash *salt*. Bring to boiling; reduce heat. Simmer, uncovered, about 15 minutes or till fruit is tender and chutney is desired consistency, stirring occasionally.

*Nutrition information per serving: 337 calories, 23 g protein, 40 g carbohydrate, 11 g fat (2 g saturated), 59 mg cholesterol, 384 mg sodium.*

# Chicken & Prosciutto Roll-Ups

*This pretty dish takes the Italian technique braciola—thin slices of meat wrapped around savories such as Italian ham, cheese, artichokes, spinach, and herbs—and applies it to chicken. Serve the attractive spirals with spinach fettuccine. (Also pictured on the cover.)*

¼ cup dry white wine
2 teaspoons snipped fresh thyme or
　　½ teaspoon dried thyme, crushed
4 medium skinless, boneless chicken
　　breast halves (about 1 pound
　　total)
4 thin slices prosciutto (about
　　1 ounce total), trimmed of fat
2 ounces fontina cheese, thinly sliced
½ of a 7-ounce jar roasted red sweet
　　peppers, cut into thin strips
　　(about ½ cup)
　　Fresh thyme sprigs (optional)

For sauce, in a small bowl combine wine and the snipped fresh or dried thyme. Set aside.

Rinse chicken; pat dry with paper towels. Place each chicken half between 2 pieces of plastic wrap. Working from center to edges, pound lightly with the flat side of a meat mallet into a rectangle about ⅛ inch thick. Remove plastic wrap.

Place a slice of prosciutto and one-fourth of the cheese on each chicken piece. Arrange one-fourth of the roasted peppers on cheese near the bottom edge of chicken. Fold in the sides; roll up jelly-roll style. Secure with wooden toothpicks. (At this point, chicken may be individually wrapped in plastic wrap and chilled up to 4 hours.)

Grill chicken on an uncovered grill directly over medium coals for 15 to 17 minutes or till tender and no longer pink, turning to cook evenly and brushing twice with sauce. Remove the toothpicks. If desired, garnish with fresh thyme sprigs. Makes 4 servings.

*Nutrition information per serving: 214 calories, 27 g protein, 2 g carbohydrate, 9 g fat (4 g saturated), 76 mg cholesterol, 294 mg sodium.*

# Chicken in a Pita

*Other wrappers also work well for this filling—try warm flour tortillas or a more traditional soft roll.*

12 ounces skinless, boneless chicken
    breast halves
 2 tablespoons olive oil or cooking oil
½ teaspoon dried oregano, crushed
¼ teaspoon salt
¼ teaspoon garlic powder
¼ teaspoon coarsely ground pepper
 4 lettuce leaves
 4 8-inch pita bread rounds
 1 small tomato, chopped
½ cup bean sprouts
    Cucumber Yogurt Sauce

Rinse chicken; pat dry with paper towels. Brush the chicken with 1 tablespoon of the oil. In a small bowl combine the oregano, salt, garlic powder, and pepper; sprinkle over chicken.

In a large skillet cook chicken in the remaining hot oil over medium heat for 8 to 10 minutes or till chicken is tender and no longer pink, turning once. Cool slightly; cut into thin strips.

Place lettuce on pita bread. Top with chicken, tomato, and bean sprouts. Drizzle with Cucumber Yogurt Sauce. Fold pitas in half and wrap with a paper napkin to secure. Serve immediately. Makes 4 sandwiches.

**Cucumber Yogurt Sauce:** In a small mixing bowl combine ½ cup *plain fat-free yogurt*; ¼ cup chopped, seeded *cucumber*; 1 tablespoon finely chopped *onion*; 1 tablespoon snipped *parsley*; ½ teaspoon *lemon juice*; and ⅛ teaspoon *garlic powder*. Cover and chill sauce till serving time.

*Nutrition information per serving: 285 calories, 23 g protein, 26 g carbohydrate, 10 g fat (2 g saturated), 45 mg cholesterol, 423 mg sodium.*

## Olive Oil Options

All olive oils are not the same. This versatile oil, made from pressed olives, is sold by grade from "pure" (a blend of lower- and higher-quality oils) to "extra virgin" (the richest in aroma and flavor). Color also indicates a flavor difference. Green to greenish gold olive oil tastes slightly sharp. Golden olive oil has a more delicate flavor.

# Warm Chicken Spinach Salad

*This refreshing main-dish salad is perfect for summertime entertaining.*

| | |
|---|---|
| 6 | cups torn spinach |
| 2 | cups torn leaf lettuce |
| 2 | red and/or green sweet peppers, cut into bite-size strips |
| 1 | medium red onion, thinly sliced |
| 12 | ounces skinless, boneless chicken breast halves |
| ½ | teaspoon dried rosemary, crushed |
| ½ | teaspoon lemon-pepper seasoning |
| 1 | clove garlic, minced |
| 1 | tablespoon cooking oil |
| 2 | tablespoons balsamic vinegar |
| 2 | tablespoons water |
| | Fresh rosemary sprigs (optional) |

In a large salad bowl combine spinach, leaf lettuce, sweet pepper strips, and sliced red onion. Cover and chill up to 2 hours.

Rinse chicken; pat dry with paper towels. Cut chicken into bite-size strips. Toss chicken with dried rosemary and lemon-pepper seasoning.

In a 10-inch skillet cook and stir chicken strips and garlic in hot oil over medium-high heat for 2 to 3 minutes or till chicken is tender and no longer pink. Remove chicken from skillet. Add to salad mixture.

For dressing, add vinegar and water to skillet; stir to scrape up any browned bits. Pour over salad. Toss to coat. Transfer to individual salad plates. If desired, garnish with fresh rosemary. Makes 4 servings.

*Nutrition information per serving: 172 calories, 20 g protein, 10 g carbohydrate, 6 g fat (1 g saturated), 45 mg cholesterol, 248 mg sodium.*

# Chicken Salad with Raspberry Vinaigrette

*If you like, arrange all the ingredients on a large glass salad plate and pass the dressing in a small cruet.*

2 cups torn leaf lettuce
2 cups torn radicchio
2 cups torn arugula
1 medium Belgian endive, cut up
4 medium skinless, boneless chicken breast halves (about 1 pound total)
1 tablespoon Dijon-style mustard
1 tablespoon honey
¼ teaspoon salt
⅛ teaspoon pepper
2 medium oranges, peeled and sliced
1 avocado, halved, seeded, peeled, and sliced lengthwise
1 pink grapefruit, peeled and sectioned
2 green onions, thinly bias sliced
Raspberry Vinaigrette
Raspberries (optional)

In a large bowl combine the leaf lettuce, radicchio, arugula, and Belgian endive. Toss lightly to mix. Cover and chill up to 2 hours.

Rinse chicken; pat dry with paper towels. For sauce, combine Dijon-style mustard, honey, salt, and pepper; set aside. Grill chicken on an uncovered grill directly over medium coals for 12 to 15 minutes or till tender and no longer pink, turning once. Brush with sauce during the last 2 minutes of grilling. Cool chicken slightly; slice into thin strips.

Arrange the greens on individual salad plates. Top with chicken strips, oranges, avocado slices, grapefruit sections, and green onions. Drizzle salads with some of the Raspberry Vinaigrette. If desired, garnish with raspberries. Makes 4 servings.

**Raspberry Vinaigrette:** In a blender container combine one 10-ounce package *frozen red raspberries,* thawed; 2 tablespoons *olive oil* or *salad oil;* 2 tablespoons *lemon juice;* and 1 clove *garlic,* minced. Cover and blend till smooth. Use a sieve to strain dressing; discard seeds. Cover and chill dressing till serving time. Reserve any remaining dressing for another use.

*Nutrition information per serving: 331 calories, 25 g protein, 26 g carbohydrate, 15 g fat (1 g saturated), 59 mg cholesterol, 295 mg sodium.*

# INDEX

# Easy Everyday Recipe Library
## MASTER INDEX

Number before the slash refers to volume number, and number after the slash refers to page number in that volume.

Casseroles

Cheese

Cheese (continued)

## TESTING RECIPES FOR PERFECT RESULTS

In the Better Homes and Gardens® Test Kitchen, we're serious about great taste and proper nutrition—so much so, in fact, that we test and retest every recipe until we're sure it will turn out perfectly every time.

Since 1928, the Test Kitchen has painstakingly tested each recipe published in all of the Better Homes and Gardens® publications, ensuring that it meets high-quality standards. Our home economists work in kitchens equipped with the same appliances you have at home, perfecting recipes so you don't have to.

After our home economists prepare each recipe, they present the dish to a panel of peers and food editors, who judge the recipe according to strict criteria. You can cook with assurance knowing that we're looking for perfect taste, texture, and appearance. To ensure it will work well for you, we also evaluate each recipe to make sure it meets the following guidelines:
- Instructions are clear, using standard, easy-to-follow cooking methods and terms.
- Cooking times, preparation instructions, and serving sizes are realistic.
- The recipe is made from ingredients that are readily available across the country and includes suggestions for substituting one ingredient for another.
- If applicable, the recipe includes timesaving methods, such as the use of prepackaged or convenience ingredients.
- When possible, the recipe calls for an entire can or package of an ingredient to avoid waste.

Thanks to our Test Kitchen, you can trust all the foods in the *Easy Everyday Recipe Library* to meet your high standards for excellent flavor, ease of preparation, and balanced nutrition.


## NUTRITION INFORMATION—HOW TO MAKE IT WORK FOR YOU

With each recipe, we give you useful nutrition information you easily can apply to your own needs. First, see "What You Need" to determine your dietary requirements. Then, refer to the nutrition information listed with each recipe. Here, you'll find the calorie count of each serving and the amount of protein, carbohydrate, fat, saturated fat, cholesterol, and sodium for each serving (see "How We Analyze"). To be more accurate, follow the suggested number of servings.

**What You Need**
These guidelines suggest nutrient levels that moderately active adults should strive to eat each day. As your calorie levels change, adjust your fat intake, too. Try to keep the percentage of calories from fat to no more than 30 percent. There's no harm in occasionally going over or under these guidelines, but the key to good health is maintaining a balanced diet most of the time.
- Calories: About 2,000
- Carbohydrate: About 300 grams
- Fat: Less than 65 grams
- Saturated Fat: Less than 20 grams
- Cholesterol: Less than 300 milligrams
- Sodium: Less than 2,400 milligrams

**How We Analyze**
Our Test Kitchen uses a computer analysis of each recipe to determine the nutritional value of a single serving. Here's how:
- The analysis does not include optional ingredients.
- We use the first serving size listed when a range is given.
- When ingredient choices appear in a recipe (such as margarine or butter), we use the first one mentioned for analysis. The ingredient order does not mean we prefer one ingredient over another.
- When milk is an ingredient in a recipe, the analysis is calculated using reduced-fat milk.